I'd like to tell you what they are

The Mysteries of Zigomar

Allan Ahlberg

THE
MYSTERIES
of
ZIGOMAR

POEMS and STORIES

Illustrated by
John Lawrence

WALKER BOOKS
AND SUBSIDIARIES
LONDON • BOSTON • SYDNEY

For Vanessa,
Amelia and David

First published 1997 by Walker Books Ltd
87 Vauxhall Walk, London SE11 5HJ

10 9 8 7 6 5 4 3 2 1

Text © 1997 Allan Ahlberg
Illustrations © 1997 John Lawrence

This book has been typeset in Monotype Garamond.

Printed in Italy

British Library Cataloguing in Publication Data
A catalogue record for this book is available
from the British Library.

ISBN 0-7445-5531-0

CONTENTS

A Cock and Bull Story

I am going to tell you a story now that will surely flabbergast you. At least, I hope it will flabbergast you. After all, it is good to be flabbergasted once in a while, if you ask me. ("Flabbergast" is one of my favourite words, by the way.)

The story is all about a cock and – you guessed it – a bull who lived together on a farm. Actually, only the bull lived there to begin with. Then the cockerel arrived and there was trouble.

Some believe it was the bull's fault. He was a bully, they say, and bull-headed besides. Others blame the cockerel. For my part, I am not sure. After all, nothing (or perhaps I should say, hardly anything) is clear cut in this life, is it? I mean, you take the biggest dwarf and the littlest giant, and they could be twins!  Anyway, judge for yourself. This is what happened.

First we have this bull (named Horace, I believe) living in quiet contentment on the farm. Well, you would expect it to be quiet really. He was the only animal there. It was a bull farm. You see, in those days the world was organized differently. Everything was more … specialized. So there were bull farms and horse farms and horseradish farms; toothpaste, shops and toothbrush shops; "Marks" on one side of the road, "Spencer" on the other, and so on. On a larger scale, there were countries where it never rained – or never stopped – or was always half-past three in the afternoon. There was even one place, much loved by cyclists and skiers, where whichever way you went it was always downhill.

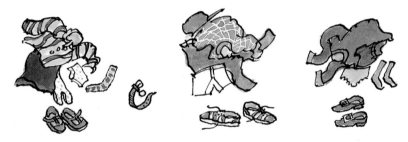

Families were specialized too. I mean, you know how quickly children grow out of their shoes or coats, for instance. What a waste it is when things that are almost brand-new cease to fit. Well, how they solved this problem then was to leave the shoes (or whatever) where they were, and change the children. When you got too big for your clothes, you simply wrapped yourself up in a towel and ran next door to where the six-year-olds or nine-year-olds (or whoever) lived, and so on, right the way up the street. It was quite logical really.

Anyway, where was I? Yes … there was the bull living in quiet contentment, when suddenly – bang!

– one day, uninvited and unannounced (except for a "Cock-a-doodle-do!", which hardly counts), in comes the cockerel. (His name was Horace too.)

This cockerel, it must be said, was conceited. He had a habit of looking down his beak at other animals, and reckoned (understandably, I suppose) that he was cock of the walk. He also had this theory that the sun came up each morning just to hear him crow. Naturally, as soon as the bull heard

this, which was pretty soon, he felt bound to disagree. The cockerel's theory was all back to front. It was the most cock-eyed thing he'd ever heard. (Actually, I can tell you now, the bull was wrong. In those days the sun *did* come up to hear the cock crow.)

So then there was a big row, as you might expect. Eventually, the bull bet the cockerel that he couldn't crow the sun up in the middle of the night. Whereupon, the cockerel said he could – and, of course, later on he did – and after that the farmer came running out.

By the way, I've just thought, I don't believe I told you why there was only the one bull on the farm.

It's simple really: bulls were expensive and one was all the farmer could afford. (Actually, half was all he could afford; he was sharing the bull with a neighbour.)

You see, that was another thing about those days: prices were dreadful. For instance, you could not buy a teddy for less than £850. A tube of Smarties was £115, and even a penny-chew cost £30. Still, high prices are not the worst thing that can happen, are they? I mean, you may not know this, but there was once a time when there was no colour in the world. Things were just black and white or shades of grey; grey skies, grey grass, grey sausages even. There were no rosy cheeks or suntans, no traffic lights come to that.

And before that there was a time when there was no shape in the world. Cats were not cat-shaped, or dogs dog-shaped. Everything was just a sort of blob, even the people. There were men blobs and women blobs. The women blobs (most of them, anyway) carried handbag blobs to tell them apart. And before *that*, believe it or not, there was a time when there was no *time*; no clocks, no calendars, no punctuality. In those days – although there were no days, come to think of it – you could not run a four-minute mile or boil an egg.

Anyway, enough of this, where was I? Yes ... the farmer came running out. Well, he was hopping mad to be woken up at such a time, as you can imagine, and threatened to knock the cockerel into a cocked hat, blacken the bull's eye and much else besides. Gradually, however, things calmed down and the farmer went back to bed, even though it was broad daylight. The bull did the decent thing and paid his bet, about six-and-a-half-thousand pounds, I believe. The cockerel did *his* best not to strut too much.

Which, I suppose, brings us to the end of the story. It only remains for me to say, I hope you have enjoyed it and been, perhaps, a little "flabbergasted" here and there. Incidentally, one last thing: the farmer's name was Horace too. I know this sounds unlikely, but there you are. (Horace is one of my favourite names, by the way.)

GETTING UP FOR SCHOOL

I'm getting up for school
Getting up for school
Getting, getting
Up for, up for
Soft-boiled egg and steamy cup for
Getting up for school.

I'll soon be up for school
Soon be up for school
Soon be leaping
Striding (creeping!)
Bye-bye boring beds and sleeping
Out and off to school.

I'm nearly up for school
Nearly up for school
Nearly (really!)
Out of bed for
Rise and shine your sleepy head for
Leave that snug and steamy bed for
Steamy, dreamy soft-boiled bed for
Bed for, bed for...

Won't be long now
Get – get – getting
In a minute
Up – up – up
Just a jiffy ... Ah! *(yawn)*
For school.

UNCLES' END

I am the ghost of Uncle Bill
If I hadn't died I'd be here still.
I miss the wife, I miss the cat
And I wish they'd buried me in my hat
For the wind blows through you
When you're a ghost.
Yes, I reckon I miss my hat the most.

I am the ghost of Uncle Joe
We may have to die but we don't have to go.
I miss my mates and my cup of tea
And watching football on TV
Liverpool – nil, West Brom – three.
I miss the Queen and the Union Jack
And I wish they'd buried me in my mac
For the damp goes through you
When you're a ghost.
Yes, I fancy I miss my mac the most.

I am the ghost of Uncle Ben
I'd rather be back in my home again.
I've got things to do, like painting the fence
Who thought of dying, it makes no sense.
I miss my mower, I miss my drill
I never did fix that windowsill.
I miss my dog – he was only a pup –
And I *do* wish they'd buried me standing up
For I feel so idle just lying here
Month after month and year after year.
It's the waste of it all I hate the most.
Yes, life's a dead loss . . .

                    when you end up a ghost.

Come here

Come here

Come here!

Come *here!*

COME HERE

COME HERE!

Coooome here!

Coooome heeeere!

C'mere!

Come … here

Come here

THE DOG WHO WOULDN'T COME

FOR I WILL CONSIDER

For I will consider my class of thirty-four children.
For they are the best (well, second-best) class
    in the whole school.
For it is a small school.
For they are full of melodrama and romance.
For they appreciate the magic of twins.
For they do as they are told (now and then)
    (some of them).
For they can enjoy a midnight feast at 9.45 p.m.
For they think that thirteen is a considerable age.
For they love doing jobs.
For they have little brothers and sisters
    in the Infants (who are *worse*).
For they believe that you can get a dry sock
    onto a wet foot.
For they are shy when they meet me out of school.
For they admire the boy who can draw like Rolf Harris.
For they make personal remarks.
For they are cruel to each other on the subjects
    of new glasses and untrendy haircuts.
For they pick up things they find in the street.

For they are fascinated by babies.

For they have secret worries.

For they are transparently crafty.

For they are interested in having their ears pierced.

For, according to their mothers, they are not
like this at home.

For they are eleven years old individually and
three hundred and seventy-four years old altogether.

For they are all different – even the twins;
especially the twins.

For they can be enraptured by a free gift in a
Sugar Puffs' packet.

For I like some of them more than others,
which I keep a secret.

For they *know*, anyway.

For they are leaving next term for a bigger and
better school, or so they believe.

For I will miss them.

For they will come back and see me, by and by,
in their new shoes and lopsided ties.

For by then the spell will be broken.

THE PAPER BOY

There was once a boy who was made out of paper; newspaper mostly, plus pages from various books and comics, a couple of envelopes, a small amount of brown paper and a sweet wrapper or two.

He was dreadfully thin, this boy – well, flat, really – and inclined to blow away in the wind. Rain was even more of a problem. It made him soggy and caused his printer's ink to run, and *him* to run as well, back into the house, school, shop doorway or whatever.

How the Paper Boy came to be made is hard to say, though it does appear that scissors and glue were used. But *when* he was made is known, more or less.

You see, the dates of two or three of the newspapers used in his construction were clearly visible: 12th March 1956, 13th March 1956, and 13th March again, which is a pretty good clue, if you ask me.

The Paper Boy led a sad and lonely life. He lived in an empty house, where presumably he had been born, or delivered, you might say. He attended the local school but had no friends. The other children would not play with him. He could not kick a ball or catch one, and was always blowing away just when you needed him.

The bullies in that school – two girls and a boy – were especially unkind. They menaced him with scissors behind the teacher's back and, on one occasion, chased him in the playground with a cigarette lighter!

Eventually, and quite unfairly, the Paper Boy was expelled from school for cheating in a history exam. It was claimed he had the answers written all over him. After that he spent much of his time at home. During the day, he would stand at the sitting-room window staring out into the street. At night he lay on his bed and read himself (yes, *himself*) to sleep. Soon he knew whole paragraphs of himself by heart, and back to front and upside down as well. He used a mirror on a stick, for instance, to read a recipe for macaroni cheese over his left shoulder ("Take a pound and a half of fresh pasta..."). The mirrors on the dressing-table revealed, at a certain angle to each other, part of a poem that the Paper Boy became especially fond of:

"Where the pools are bright and deep,
Where the grey trout lies asleep,
Up the river and over the lea,
That's the way for Billy and me."

And the Paper Boy, in the emptiness of his house, would think, "Wish *I* was Billy. Hm ... wish I was 'Me'."

Now and then, when the weather was fine and not too windy, the Paper Boy went out. He wandered around the shopping precinct or sat on a bench in the park. His thoughts in those days, for much of the time, were taken up with Pinocchio. His teacher had read the story of Pinocchio to the whole class earlier in the year. The truth is, the Paper Boy loved Pinocchio: a wooden boy – a puppet, really – who yearned to become a real boy, and who was bold and had adventures, got swallowed by a whale and so on – and won! And the Paper Boy, in the ordinariness and flatness of his own life, would think, "Hm ... if only."

Then one day once more the bullies got him. They cornered him in the park – just the two girls this time, Jennifer and Caroline their names were – and did dreadful things to him. In the space of ten short minutes, they picked him up and knocked him down a dozen times, ate their fish and chips off him, tried flying him like a kite, wiped their *feet*

on him, *screwed him up into a ball* (oh, poor Paper Boy, it's like a horror movie!) and tossed him into a litter bin. After that, Caroline said something nasty about Jennifer and the two of them went running off, no doubt to bully each other.

Silence. A breeze rustled the grass, ducks quacked on the far side of the park, traffic hummed. Then more rustling and a curious sort of creaking, but this time from inside the litter bin.

Moments later a paper hand appeared at the edge of the bin, and then another. Painfully, pitifully, the Paper Boy emerged, heaved himself out of the bin and toppled down onto the grass. His legs were still all crumpled up; he looked a bit like Toulouse-Lautrec, the famous short-legged painter. His face was crumpled too, which affected his eyesight. Wherever he looked, it seemed the world was *rippling* around him, as though it was underwater.

The Paper Boy sat on the grass and stared forlornly across the park. He relived the sensation of being scrunched up, as though into some preposterous yoga position.

He thought of the school, the bullies with their cigarette lighter, that recipe for macaroni cheese. He thought of his empty house and even emptier life. He thought … of Pinocchio.

The Paper Boy began to move. He smoothed out his legs and flattened his face to the best of his ability. He stood up. A sudden flood of hopefulness surged through him. There was little prospect of *his* becoming a "real boy", but so what? He was a paper boy; mere tearable, crushable, *combustible* paper, and proud of it.

By now the evening sunlight was slanting across the grass. Resolutely, the Paper Boy left the park and strode off towards the bustling streets.

Months went by. The Paper Boy decorated his house, inside and out, in more cheerful colours. He planted seeds and bulbs and little shrubs in the garden. He adopted two stray cats. By a lucky chance, he discovered a fifty-pound note in one of those envelopes he was partly made from. This came in handy when buying the paint, cat food and so on. Also, he got a job.

Three mornings a week, the Paper Boy worked as an assistant in the nearby (Wallace Avenue) nursery school. He was especially helpful with the cleverer of the four- and five-year-olds who were learning to read. He was the most popular book in the place.

The children liked to colour him in as well. They put colour in his cheeks, gave him some blue shoes and filled in his "o's". They gave him some hair too.

The Paper Boy lay patiently on a big table while all this colour was being applied. The fat wax crayons tickled somewhat and often he laughed out loud. That afternoon when he went home, his amiable cats ("Billy" and "Me") had trouble recognizing him.

Years went by. The Paper Boy began to work four mornings a week at Wallace Avenue. One of his cats (Billy!) had kittens. His garden blossomed and bloomed.

It was nine o'clock on a warm spring morning. The Paper Boy – well, teenager now – came staggering into Mrs Morgan's class with a cardboard box. The children rushed to help with the box and

open it up. It contained a great accumulation of paper: newspaper and magazines, silver paper, wallpaper, Christmas wrapping paper, till receipts, bus tickets; also some falling-apart books: Charles Dickens, Roald Dahl, Topsy and Tim. Yes, the variety was considerable. The Paper Boy had been collecting for weeks.

Mrs Morgan produced pots of glue and pairs of lightweight plastic scissors. She chose four ecstatic children to work with the Paper Boy and took twelve grumpy ones away to work with her. The Paper Boy and his assistants transferred the piles of paper and books to the table. The work began.

This piece here, that piece there. This piece ... here – no, there! That piece ... hm, I'm not sure yet. Pass the scissors! That's upside down – I've gone all wrong – that's back to front! That's ... lovely.

Three hours later, when most of the other children were getting their coats on to go home, the

Paper Boy and his helpers finished their work. Yes, there she was – you've guessed it, I suppose – with her Christmas-paper skirt and crayoned smile, ginger freckles and dangly earrings, Roald Dahl legs and shiny-paper shoes: the Paper Girl.

The Paper Girl sat up and looked around. She seemed bewildered, which was hardly surprising. The Paper Boy was speechless (the children, of course, were anything but). A rush of shyness almost overwhelmed him. His paper brain was in a turmoil, his paper heart was full. Nevertheless, his hopes were high and he was quite prepared to be adventurous, should the need arise.

Pinocchio would have been proud of him.

WHERE I SIT WRITING

Where I sit writing I can see
A page, a pen, a line or three
Of scribbled verse; a cup of tea.

A spider's web, a window pane,
A garden blurred a bit with rain,
A low and leaden sky; a plane.

Where I sit writing I can see
An evening sky, a sodden tree,
A window pane reflecting ... me.

Out in the garden's fading light,
Departing day, approaching night,
He copies every word I write.

Where I sit writing I can see
A hand, a pen, a verse or three;
A distant road; a cup – no tea.

A list of rhymes, some crossings out,
Confusions, choices, doodles, doubt.
No clue to what it's all about.

Where I sit writing I can see
A glowing sky, a darkened tree,
Some Sellotape, a saucer ... me.

THE FILLING STATION

(COUNTRY STYLE)

The word is spreadin' across the nation,
Git your kids to the Fillin' Station.
Teachers now can take their ease
While moms and dads say, "Fill 'em up, please!"

Fill 'em up with Maths and Readin'.
Anythin' more, Ma'am, you'll be needin'?
Spanish, German, History?
Half a dozen subjects and y'get one free.

Attach these wires to your wrist,
Relax here on this special bed,
Shut y'eyes and don't resist,
Feel that education flowin' into your head.

C'mon down to the Fillin' Station,
We're gonna build a new generation.
How 'bout the toddler? Only three?
Soon he'll be a little infant prodigy.

Forget about your sand 'n' water,
Teach him all those things y'oughter.
Shakespeare, Dickens, Roald Dahl too;
Literature is good for you.

Place these goggles over his eyes,
Lay him in this little cot,
Golden slumbers, big surprise,
When he wakes up, he'll know the lot.

In one ear and in the other.
Could y'use a top up for his older brother?
Seems a bit empty, if'n you ask me.
Have y'ever thought about a PhD?

No more learnin', no more books,
No more tough exams to pass.
No more teachers' grumpy looks,
Soon we'll *all* be top of the class.

Just got back from the Fillin' Station,
We're gonna have a big celebration.
Kids all sittin' in a row,
Ain't a blessed thing that they don't know.

Name that wind in the South of France.
What's the square of minus eight?
Is it true that bees can dance?
Who wrote a show called "Kiss Me Kate"?
Where do whales and penguins thrive?
What's the longest river in Tennessee?
Will the human race survive…?
Y'all know the answers – and so do we!

Yippee!

The word is spreadin' across the nation,
Git your kids to the Fillin' Station.
Collect them tokens, don't be dumb;
Albert Einstein, here – we – come!

FATHER AND CHILD

Upon that sharp and frosty eve
Muffled in scarf and glove
With frosty snow beneath their feet
And frosty sky above:
A father and his child.

Climbing the narrow hilly street
With letters in their hands
And Christmas cards and packets too
To where the postbox stands.
The child runs on ahead.

A cautious car comes ghosting by
An ebb and flow of light.
Somewhere an ice-cream van chimes out
Ice-cream on such a night!
The child, though, would like one.

The father raises up his face
He stares into the sky
And marvels at the myriad stars
And hears his child reply:
It's like a join-the-dots.

Back down the hill, now hand-in-hand
Father and child return
While overhead and unobserved
The frosty heavens burn.
And the child thinks: Ice-cream!

The Vampire and the Hound

Towards the distant mountains flying,
Closer, closer,
In darkness, wind and rain;
Above the ancient castle sighing,
Nearer, nearer,
The Vampire comes again.

In at my Lady's window staring,
Closer, closer,
His pale eyes calm and dead,
Watching the beeswax candle flaring,
Nearer, nearer,
Beside my Lady's bed.

Over the golden carpet going,
Closer, closer,
His black cloak furled and wet,
Up to the bed where, all unknowing,
Nearer, nearer,
My Lady's sleeping yet.

Come at last to his monstrous calling,
Closer, closer,
Unchecked by keep or moat,
The Vampire, swooning low and falling,
Nearer, nearer,
Towards my Lady's throat.

Wakes to a nightmare foul, and screaming,
Murder, murder!
My Lady, silken-gowned.
Up from the hearth-rug, damply steaming,
Save her, save her!
Lottie, my Lady's Hound.

Black night and rain at the windows lashing,
Louder, louder,
Warm blood upon the floor,
Blood on the silken sheets a-splashing,
Redder, redder,
Blows on the bolted door.

The savaged Vampire, faint and fleeing,
Horror, horror!
The sundered door gapes wide.
Servants aghast at the sight they're seeing;
Save us, save us!
The Hound with a bleeding side.

My Lady there at the bedside kneeling,
Weeping, weeping,
Stroking her saviour's head.
Fire-thrown shapes on the distant ceiling,
Higher, higher,
And Lottie, the brave dog … dead.

THE FIRE ESCAPE

Long, long ago there was no fire and consequently no hot water, toasted tea cakes or warm slippers. Think of that! Then, one day a man – or maybe it was a woman; yes, it *was* a woman, now I come to think – invented matches, and life at once became altogether more ... cosy.

The woman who invented the matches kept them in a paper bag in her apron pocket. (No, not a paper bag, paper bags hadn't been invented then. It must have been something else.) Unfortunately, one day, while trying to collect some frog spawn for her little boy,  she fell in the river and the matches were ruined.

Well, the woman was doubly unhappy about this, even though, as it turned out, her pocket was full of frog spawn, which pleased her little boy no end. She was wet through for one thing, and not sure she could invent the matches again for another. You see, really the first time it was just a lucky accident. She had been trying to invent a pencil-sharpener. Or was it a pencil? No – pencil-sharpener, definitely.

Then, that night, something worse happened: the fire escaped. I should explain that there was just the one fire – started some weeks earlier with the woman's matches – which the village shared. I should also explain that fire was a little different in those days. It was, well … *wilder*. Actually, most things were wilder then.

The dogs were wilder, the cows were wilder – there was no milk, for instance; the cows were for ever kicking the milk pails over – even the flowers were wilder.

Anyway, there it is, the fire was wilder and it escaped.

The next morning, after much complaining from their husbands about cold shaving water and cold tea (it was bad enough there was no milk), the woman and a few of her friends chased after the fire. They caught it soon enough. Its trail, as you can imagine, was easy to follow and, even when its flame burned low and it tried to hide, the smoke gave it away.

However, catching up with a fire is one thing, getting it home again is another. I believe that if that woman had not there and then invented the first fire bucket, this story would have stopped stone dead. But, luckily, she did and we can keep going.

So, where was I?

Yes …

the fire.

The fire was returned to its open-air pit in the middle of the village. A day or so later a young man was given the job of keeping an eye on it. He was the first fire-guard, I suppose. And that, more or less, is it.

I should tell you, by the way, that the woman never did manage to invent matches again. She had no luck with the pencil-sharpener either. But she did invent one other thing, at least: the first fishing net. She made it out of one of her old nylon stockings. (Did I tell you she invented stockings? Well, she did.) Now her little boy can set to and catch his own frog spawn, while his bone-dry mother dozes on the bank.

Actually, he is getting to be quite a big boy these days, and something of a handful. (Did I mention that *children* were wilder then? Well, they were.) His mother blames the school, or rather will do, just as soon as she invents it.

GIDDYING

Spin on the grass and shut your eyes
Feel the Earth a-turning.

Shut your eyes and fall on the grass
Feel the pull of the Earth.

Fall on the grass and lie on the grass
Feel the Earth a-tilting.

Lie on the grass and look at the sky
Feel the curve of the Earth.

Look at the sky and look at your watch
Feel the Earth a-fading.

Look at your watch and hurry home
In time for tea.

THE ACTOR'S MOTHER

No charming chatty Prince for him,
Lines by the yard.
He mostly stands there with a spear:
My son, the guard.

He never plays the Captain's part,
Always the crew.
"Aye, aye!" he cries, occasionally.
His lines are few.

He doesn't get the better roles,
Takes after me.
Sometimes he never speaks at all:
My son, the tree.

The only time he got some lines,
Just half a page,
He had to shout them through a door,
Invisibly – off stage!

Still, curtains fall eventually,
And homeward in the car
His dad and I can then admire:
Our son, the star.

Cemetery Road

When I was a boy
Just nine years old,
We moved to a house
On Cemetery Road.

The road was rough
Not well-to-do.
It split
The cemetery in two.

On winter nights
The gravestones glowed
In streetlamp shine
On Cemetery Road.

When coming home
My heart would beat
From footsteps
That were not my feet.

On frosty evenings
Scared to death
By breathing
That was not my breath.

Until at times
I'd quite explode
And run for my life
Down Cemetery Road.

Along the entry,
Velvet black,
Into the house
And not look back.

Yet now, alas,
My pulse has slowed.
I'm quite grown up.
It's just a road.

WORLDS

The first world
Was made of paper.
God screwed it up in a ball.
It would not do at all.

The second world
Was made of ice-cream,
Fudge flavour mostly,
In a delicate (8000-mile diameter) wafer cup.
God ate it up.

The third world
Was made of modelling clay.
God baked it in the oven
And gave it to his grandma.

The ninth world
Was made of house bricks,
Artfully arranged.
God won second prize
In a competition with it.

The twelfth world
Was made – woven, actually –
Of magic-carpet material.
It commuted between here and there.
There were two billion
Uncomplicated if somewhat wind-blown
People on it.

The thirteenth world
Was perfect.
God put it down somewhere
And has been looking for it
Ever since.

The twenty-fifth world
Was made of a miraculous new substance
With mind-boggling properties.
It had an unfortunate smell, though,
Like rarely-opened wardrobes.

The thirtieth world
Was made of dirt and water
Day and night
Grass
Trees
Bungalows
Odd socks
Incomplete jigsaw puzzles
Volcanoes
Fluff
Happiness and boredom
Wedding rings
General elections
Telephone books
And me and you.

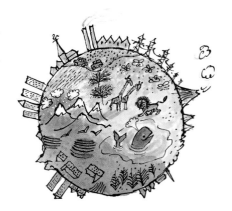

God said that it would do.

Snow White Lies

*I*t *was the middle of winter.*

No, it wasn't.

A certain queen sat working at a window.

Hardly.

She pricked her finger and three drops of blood fell on the snow.

No again. I mean – *snow*? Indoors? This was supposed to be a palace!

The Queen spoke: "Would that I might bear a child with skin as white as this snow, cheeks as red as this blood and hair as black as this window frame."

Well, what can I say? No, no, *no*! Snow White, let's be clear about this, was a red-head. There are photographs to prove it; sepia photographs, it's true, but her *freckles* are as plain as day.

Snow White grew up and the Queen died. That bit's true; knocked down by the royal coach, actually.[1] After a while the King remarried. The new queen, despite what you have heard, was a harmless woman, if somewhat eccentric. She had a

---

[1] And the King was driving; now there *is* a story.

tendency to talk to herself, particularly when sitting in front of a mirror. But there was no *magic* mirror, no magic anything. The Queen asked the questions: **"Mirror, mirror on the wall"** – dressing-table, more like – and the *Queen* answered them.

So what about all the rest, you ask: the Queen's rage, Snow White abandoned in the forest, the Seven Dwarfs and all that. *Seven Dwarfs* – ha! – five, more like, and not all dwarfs either. One of them was six foot three.

Let me tell you something about dwarfs. Here's a quote: "God produced the dwarfs because the mountains lay waste and useless, and valuable stores of silver and gold were concealed in them. He made the dwarfs right wise and crafty –" (some of them) "– that they could distinguish good and bad, and to what use all things should be applied."[2]

You see, the truth is those dwarfs weren't just a bunch of little blokes bamboozled by a nine-year-old (or thirteen, or whatever she was). In those days, dwarfs were *highly* regarded, looked up to, you might say. They had status.

Anyway, back to the so-called story. The Queen: **"Take Snow White away into the wide wood that I might never see her more."** And later on, a servant: **"I will not hurt thee, thou pretty child."** Poppycock!

[2] *Little Big Men: A Short History of Dwarfs* (Rutter, 1904)

Then we come to the alone-in-the-woods bit: *In the evening she came to a little cottage and went in there to rest herself. Everything was spruce and neat in the cottage. On the table was spread a white cloth, and there were seven little plates with seven little loaves and seven little tankards with beer in them, and knives and forks laid in order, and by the wall stood seven little beds.*

Yes, well, take that lot with a pinch of salt. I mean, she was *there*, I'll give you that, but as for the rest, it's as full of holes as a sieve. For instance, bread and beer – what kind of meal is that? And besides, who laid the table? The dwarfs were still out working halfway up a mountain (or under it).

And so it continues: Snow White falls asleep in one of the little beds – the dwarfs return – she spins them her sob story about the "Wicked Queen" – they swallow it, hook, line and sinker.

And *that* bit, more's the pity, is true as well. "Right wise and crafty" – ha! She pulled the wool over *our* eyes, that's for sure. We – blast it! I've slipped up there. I was saving that for the end; meant to surprise you. Damn! Well, you know it now. Your storyteller (*un*-teller, more like) is a dwarf, one of the famous seven (five!) and proud of it. Not that she fooled *me*, mind. Doc, Happy, Dopey, of course, they were taken in, but I had my doubts from the beginning.

Anyway, there she was sobbing her socks off, and offering to work them off as well, if only we'd let her stay. She'd cook and wash and sweep and knit and spin and all the rest of it. And did she? No. In no time at all that cottage (spruce and neat!) was a mess, and *her* room in particular. That's where I get the idea that she was thirteen, not nine, as she claimed. I mean, she was a *teenager*.

The biggest headache was the phone bills. She must have been on that phone for hours. Yes, the dwarfs had a phone, an old-fashioned one, I'll grant you, but a phone. You see, all that "olden days" stuff was a load of twaddle as well. We had phones then – and newspapers – and photographs. Those were *scientific* times.[3]

So Snow White stayed with the dwarfs. Each morning they'd set off for work – with her still in bed – and each evening they'd return to a shambles. Her excuses were priceless. She hadn't washed up because some old woman had stuck a poisoned comb in her head. There was no tea on the table because some other old woman had laced her up too tight to breathe in a corset. A corset! She was only nine years old, according to her.

[3] And I do mean science, not all that Frankenstein bolts-in-your-neck stuff.

But now we're coming to it, the nub of the whole thing, where this entire story – rigmarole! – came from. Snow White ... made ... it ... up.

As I see it, she'd probably had some trouble with her stepmother – the usual family rows, or she was bored or whatever – and consequently ran away from home. From then on, whenever she found herself in a fix, she just talked her way out of it. One tale led to another, as it does, and before she knew what she was up to, there it was: "Snow White and the Seven Dwarfs", a work of more or less unadulterated fiction.[4]

Actually, I'm saying she made it up, but even that's not the whole of it. I mean, what's all that forest business but pure "Babes in the Wood"?

[4] Many years later, Snow White – divorced and living with her sister (yes, sister, you never hear about her) – told her "story" to a couple of brothers who subsequently included it in their collection of fairy tales. *Fairy* tales; that says it all.

And how about this? *That evening the seven little dwarfs returned to the cottage. They saw at once that all was not right.* (You can say that again.) *The first said, "Who's been sitting on my stool?" The second, "Who's been eating off my plate?" The third, "Who's been drinking my beer?" And so on, up to the seventh, "Who's been sleeping in MY bed?"*

Where have you heard *that* before? All that's missing is the porridge.

Yes, she made it up, definitely, and when she couldn't make it up, she stole it. You see, after a while, and fed up with living in a jumble sale, we got her into the local school. The school bus (horse-drawn) stopped right outside the cottage. Anyway, *Goldilocks* was in the same class. It was her she was mostly on the phone to. So, in a way, they were *all* at it. (Red Riding Hood was another.) If you ask me, half the so-called "Classics of Children's Literature"

were just this gang of melodramatic school kids trying to talk their way out of trouble. There again, they could have been having a contest: who could spin the most *implausible* story and get away with it. I mean, wolves dressed up as grandmas – ha!

Anyway, it's been my intention, after all these years (you know the saying: short legs, long life) to put the record straight, which I hope I've managed to do. There are just a few loose ends and I've finished. First, the poisoned apple: well, there wasn't one, or a glass coffin. They were just an excuse – part of the plot, as it were – to bring on ... the Prince! There's a lot of vanity tucked away in this story, you know, once you realize who the author was. Thus:

The dwarfs: ***"Good heavens, what a lovely child she is!"*** That servant (mentioned previously): ***"I will not hurt thee, thou pretty child."*** And, finally, the non-existent Prince: ***"I love thee better than all the world."***

Anyway, there you have it. Poisoned apple? Bunkum. Glass coffin? Balderdash. Handsome Prince? Wishful thinking.

The truth is, the man she really married, some years later, was a college lecturer, a Mr Derek (or Dennis) White. That's another thing, "White" was only her married name. Her maiden name, her real name, while all these amazing and romantic events were supposedly taking place, was – wait for it – *Woplington*.

Woplington. She kept that to herself. My name, by the way, in case you're wondering or haven't guessed, is Grumpy. I'm not too happy with that, of course, though I'd never dream of changing it – to *Gawain*, for instance. No, there's altogether too much fiction around here already. *Somebody* needs to stick with the truth. What more can I say?[5]

[5] *Gawain* – ha!

THE SECRETS OF THE STAFFROOM

You may well think y'knows it all,
You cheeky kids today,
But I 'ave got a tale to tell
To blow y'minds away;
About your teachers, cruel and kind,
Quick-witted, vile and slow,
And the secrets of the staffroom if ...
Y'really want to know.

Y'may suppose they sits in there
Just drinking pots of tea,
With nice triangular sandwiches
Politely as can be.
Well, that was maybe how it was
Back then, but not today.
More like it's now a crate of beer
And a Chinese take-away.

Y'might have guessed the place was full
Of markin', books and chalk;
Educational supplements
And intellectual talk.
The plays of William Shakespeare,
The exports of Brazil,
But never a pile of bettin' slips
From that well-known William Hill.

Perhaps y'thought they spend their time
With felt pens, paint and glue,
Worrying themselves to death
To do their best for you.
While some, it's true, are softies,
There's others 'ard as sin,
A-jabbin' Playdoh infants with
A nasty little pin.

There's teachers, every school has some,
Who work until they drop,
To help their lucky pupils climb
The ladder to the top.
There's others, though, with bloodshot eyes
Below a crafty frown,
Who sharpen up the staffroom axe
To chop the ladder down.

I knew a staffroom once that 'ad
A trap door in the floor,
That led down to an … awful place,
I'd rather not say more.
When governors came calling,
It always was the rule,
They never found a single
Trouble-maker in that school.

You may have wondered how I know
These things of which I speak.
Well, I was once a caretaker
For ninety quid a week.
But since I've gone and blown the gaff
And give the game away,
The staffroom mob is on my trail
And it's *me* who'll 'ave to pay.

So watch y'steps and peel y'eyes
And keep y'noses clean;
The secrets of the staffroom ain't
For all – see what I mean?
Beyond that door there lies a place
You never oughter go.
Unless, of course, you're curious and …
Y'really want to know.

THE SLOW MAN

The phone rings
But never long enough
For the Slow Man.

By the time
The set's switched on
His favourite programme's over.

His tea grows cold
From cup to lip
His soup evaporates.

He laughs, eventually,
At jokes long since
Gone out of fashion.

Sell-by dates
And limited special offers
Defeat him.

He comes home
With yesterday's paper
And reads it ... tomorrow.

The Mysteries of Zigomar

I'd like to tell you what they are
The Mysteries of Zigomar.

I think it's time to spill the beans
And spell out what the whole thing means.

Remove the mask, reveal the trail
Unbag the cat and lift the veil.

Yes, lay my cards upon the table
And see an end to myth and fable.

Say, Here it is! and, There we are!
The Mysteries of Zigomar.

No more delay, no dark confusion
Just simple facts and a conclusion.

I think it's time, I think it's late
The world has had too long to wait.

From Stoke-on-Trent to Cooch Behar
We're driven mad by Zigomar.

From long ago to times like these
One tangled web of mysteries.

But not much longer – Goodbye doubt!
The time has come to spit it out.

I'd like to tell you what they are
The Mysteries of Zigomar.

I'd like to tell, you'd *love* to hear …
The trouble is, I've no idea.

LADYBIRD

There was once a woman who turned into a bird. No magic was involved, no potions, spells or wardrobes. She just stood at the sink one morning in front of an enormous pile of washing-up from a party the night before and thought to herself, "There's more to life than washing-up," and, presently, turned into a bird and flew out of the window. So this is why the story is called "Ladybird". Actually, it could have been called "Batman", because later that same day on his way home from work the lady's husband, while stuck in a traffic jam, thought to himself, "Blow this for a game of soldiers!" and turned into a bat. He then flew off, just like his wife, leaving the car where it was and making the traffic jam even worse, incidentally.

The couple's two children, a boy aged eight and a girl aged three, managed fairly well for a time.

(Their mother flew by now and then to see how they were, though they never knew it was her.) However, eventually they became bored with making their own beds, cooking their own teas and telling their own stories. The boy thereafter turned into a hedgehog and set off to see the world, or visit his grandma at least, and the girl turned into a horse and, later on, won a number of races for three-year-olds. (Three is quite old for a horse, as the girl discovered. Come to think of it, eight is *ancient* for a hedgehog.)

So, there we are, that's one family pretty much broken up, I suppose. Mother a bird, father a bat, brother a hedgehog, sister a horse. I'd like to be able to say that they all got back together at some stage, but, of course, life, as you well realize, is not like that.

I'd like to tell you all about
The Mysteries of Fomalhaut